INEDIBLE INDELIBLES

Yearbook of Poetry 2016

All rights reserved; no part of this publication may be reproduced or transmitted by any means; electronic, mechanical, photocopying or otherwise, without the prior permission of the authors.

Poetry written by members of the Indelible Poetry Club on Allpoetry.com

Table of Contents

Title _____ 1

Copyright _____ 2

Acknowledgements _____ 8

Elegia _____ 10

   Across the Abyss (Indelible collaboration) _____ 12

   Intertwined (Collaboration with Monarch) _____ 18

   Sunset kiss (Collaboration with RJ Kram) _____ 20

Becki Friend _____ 22

   The Dancer _____ 24

   Cutting on the Bias _____ 26

   Shell Lovers _____ 28

Blue Raven _____ 29

   Venice _____ 30

   Caffè Reggio _____ 31

   On Horseback _____ 32

Danna Hobart _____ 33

   Vacancy _____ 34

   Wilted _____ 36

Summer Nights _____ 38

Dave Kavanagh _____ 40

The hardness of geometry _____ 42

Snow in Dublin City _____ 43

Rocket Ships & Shooting Stars _____ 46

Ellafonte _____ 48

I miss the curves of certain roads _____ 49

A lash let loose _____ 51

But why am I here, pulling ribbon _____ 53

Errant Panther _____ 55

Of Feathers and Faith (Vignettes) _____ 57

Take a Chance (Dasyure Form) _____ 61

Kicking Up the Rain _____ 62

Fragmented Sage _____ 64

Sounds of Silence _____ 65

Season of Joy _____ 67

My Walker _____ 68

HuesFac3 _____ 70

Diamonds _____ 71

Splash _____ 72

Wait-rose _____ 73

Irene Clasper _____ 75

She smelled like a cyclone [Vignettes] _____ 76

Whimsicalities of ordinary on a Stranger — 79

Together we are a rainbow in brume's attic — 81

James Allen — 82

Why I Love Bobby Sharp — 84

In Romania Tonight — 86

Resuscitation of the Blue Boy — 87

Linda Marshall — 89

The Porajmos — 90

Embracing Autumn — 95

For the risen Christ — 97

Mark Andrew James Terry — 99

Dreaming Springing — 100

The Econ's Fishin' Hole — 101

Morning Wok Scramble — 103

MJ Donnelly — 104

Three Fingers of Jameson Gold Reserve, Neat — 106

Ghosts Muse and Count All of Autumn's Crisp Leaves — 108

Shimmering Salvation — 109

Monarch — 110

Butterflower — 112

Longing lips — 114

पुकार — 115

MusicBoxMetaphor — 116
- Father — 117
- The Mud Room — 118
- The Following Sea — 120

Only Rob — 122
- Detritus — 123
- Speaking of Water — 125
- Welcome to the Poem Farm — 128

Paula Tohline Calhoun — 130
- À la recherché du temps perdu — 132
- Square Peg Considers Her Métier and Ponders the Alternatives — 133
- Still I Fly — 134

PoetProlific — 135
- An Old Man's Prayer — 136
- Daily Encore — 140
- Fall For It — 142

RJ Kram — 143
- A drink to regret — 145
- Watching Snow Flakes — 146
- Gone too soon — 147

Scott Waters — 149
- Outside the box — 150

If a brick wall in Chicago could talk	153
persimmon	155
Shelby Simmons	**157**
Taxi Services Don't Send Spaceships	159
April 14 (A poem)	161
This body writes poetry also	162
Skylar7	**164**
Walking Mirrors	165
2nd Degree Burns	166
Deforestation	167
Socalalto	**168**
Silverberry is Lavender Blue	170
Shadow Cat	171
Winter Woods Waiting	173
Tuni	**174**
Water Hyacinth	175
Januaryscape	176
I'm waiting for #86 by Café Fariyas	177
Word Gatherer	**178**
My Spirit Weeps the Wailing of a Thousand Years	180
The Essence of Your Soul	181
Collection	182

Acknowledgements

We wish to express our utmost gratitude to our incredibly talented writer-friends on AllPoetry.com: Kevin (its founder) and our amazing family-like poetic club, **the Indelible Poetry Club**: Achromatic, Andrew Sano, Athena1992, Becki Friend, Black Hamlet, Black Narcissus, Blue Raven, Brandon Schrumpf, Chromatic Prayer, Cp Culliton, Damian Harrowe, Danna Hobart, Dave Kavanagh, David Betzer, Disturb Infinity, Doll, Dune, Ella34, Ellafonte, Errant Panther, Espanolito, FragmentedSage, Freehope, Fric not Frac, Geneva H, Gmcookie, Gotha tway, Howard C, HuesFac3, Inverse, Irene Clasper, Jace Loring, James C. Allen, Jasmine, Just josh, Lliwen, Jean A, Jeanette P.S., Jesann, Krenna smart, Ksparrow, Kylie Jensen, LauraAnn, LilAj, Linda Marshall, Lori Hamilton, Lunalady, Margrit, Mark Andrew J Terry, Meerkatpost, MJ Donnelly, Mlou, Mockingjaye, Mumble away, MusicBoxMetaphor, MusingsInverse, Myriad-dark, Nameless-Faceless, Only rob, Paula T. Calhoun, PersephoneInWinter, Peter William, Poetdee, PoetProlific, Rahul raina, Ralfkay, RolinSton, Ron Wiseman, Scott Waters, Secarijo, Sharon H, Sharrock, Shelby Simmons, Skylar7, Socalalto, Stan A. Bryce, TheGumDealer, Tuni, Vere, Vernal, Virginia Archer, Visceral, Vito Tribuzio, Word Gatherer, Witterwax and Yehoshua Aryeh.

Elegia also thanks the two coordinators of the Indelible poetry Club: Monarch and RJ Kram.

Snatch our quills
Tear our parchments
Drain our inkwells
We
are written
everywhere

Elegia

Greetings, reader!

My name is Elegia. I live in a small picturesque village on the Hudson, Nyack; Edward Hopper's hometown and home to many writers and musicians in the Hudson Valley.

I have always enjoyed reading and writing. In fact, I could not tell you when I first started writing; I must have been writing stories in my head when I was a baby.

A few years ago, I joined AllPoetry.com to share my writing with the poetic community and a year ago, after getting to know many talented writers on AllPoetry.com, I decided to start a poetic group. After some deliberations, including very humorous ones, the group was named **the Indelible Poetry Club**. Since then it has grown close to ninety members, all gifted writers of different styles and genres.

We shared an incredible year together: wrote collaborations, hosted club contests, wrote for battles of the groups, celebrated contest winners and books published by club members, but most of all, we grew together as writers and friends. Thank you, Indelible Poetry Club, for enriching my life with your friendship and beautiful poetry!

This book is a compilation of our best poetry with biographies of the writers, a yearbook of sorts, intended to celebrate our first year together and to showcase the outstanding talent in the club. Please enjoy and if you want to find out more, read us on **AllPoetry.com** or buy this book and share it with your friends.

Across the Abyss (Indelible collaboration)

Two part collaboration from the Indelible Poetry Club. Each part consists of a Letter written from the perspective of a passenger on the Titanic and a Response from the perspective of someone who came across it in a bottle.

Letter I

The ship is sinking and there is no time to waste. The gentleman next to me was kind enough to lend me his pen and paper that I might make my goodbyes in our remaining moments. I am sorry, my dearest, but I couldn't in good conscience leap aboard a lifeboat knowing that by staying behind, I could save more lives. Who knew selflessness ran so strongly within me? Me, who hoards the books, steals the covers and takes the last of the sweets...

My only regret is...no. I won't play this game else my ire would set ablaze what the Atlantic hasn't claimed. There was to be more time! I am an unfinished painting left to rot on the ocean's floor. What good is it to know how to swim when abandoned to the middle of the frigid sea?

My only solace is you, my sweet sister. Bask beautifully in the sun of coming changes and let me, from beyond, nourish you. Stand tall my suffragette and waste not a tear! I shall watch you from heaven and send tears of joy as you grow and blossom into a beautiful woman. Relish the rain, and find me in it, always.

Fric not frac

Response I

My ship has sunk
and now I find you,
my too mortal
unfound lover.

Would that I
could be a page,
that you would write
your life upon.

I seethe at who
did take your seat,
my selfish heart
resents salvation.

All my cookies
are unpilfered,
bookshelves groan
with unread tomes.
My feet
in lonely blankets roast.

I'd reach through frozen fathoms
and a hundred years,
to see you smile.

What use endurance?
You were stolen
long before I ever was.

I think of you on sunny days
and straighten
like a hopeful suitor.

God has died
'tween then and now,
I will not cry
for you or Him.

And when I swim
on oceans deep
I know beneath's
a Masterpiece.

Andrew Sano

Letter II

In what forsaken ways peril befalls! How ironic that the devil is disguised as water - the herald of life. Cold and benumbed, my knuckles quiver as I scribe the last remaining breaths on tattered scrolls.

"Alice, oh sweet Alice! How your eyes enchant me!" I should have told her at the soirée last blue moon. She will never know now.

A feather nor a petal pink shall brush my curious fingertips. These soggy feet won't imprint upon the lands I mapped on the globe in my study. I never took that train to Paris. Nor did I ever bridle the hands on the dial. The timekeeper is callous and that lighthouse is far.

Deck lights flicker, her waist crackles, the Titan tilts. All that remains is the icy stern and broken hull, wailing mistresses and fragile, innocent tears… and the invisible offing; the offing where stars now toss like pebbles.

"Gosh, that sunset was so beautiful."

Why should I cling onto the handrail? It is so terribly easy to die. The reflection of the moon beckons me into the depths where the whales call. And I shall listen. I shall embrace the cold swells of the North. Fret I not for she is my lover. Overlapping waves lure me.

The bosom of her highest tide is where my blood shall freeze.

Monarch

Response II

Somewhere in the icy chill
of North Atlantic
your tomb is cradled
by the cold waves.
Drifting icebergs
whisper you lullabies.

A lonesome soul
who has not known sorrow
but captured the twinkle of
the first star of love
on-board the ocean's
largest tragedy.

Please believe that
a century is just a moment
before the eternity
of your loving words.

Let me fly to where
your bones are buried,
I will seek you in those
dark depths
and thrust myself
before Poseidon
begging for your release.

Let this little flicker
grow into forever stars

for I shall be your Alice
in a universe of us.

Elegia

Intertwined (Collaboration by Elegia and Monarch)

A sweet melody carves
your silhouette on gentle waves.
Alone
I lie on moonlit banks in verdant lap
of *Vrindavan*,
seeking you in flowerbeds
I whisper
to the hollow flute.

Enchanted
gopis prance around my tearful eyes
while peacocks sing.

Yet my heart wanders
to a village beyond the rustling palms
where on the swings of spring
you sway,
kissing the soul of all that breathes.

Immersed
in the warmth of your memories
I wonder if
You,
beloved Radhika,
are listening
to my tunes of love.

Monarch as Krishna

I hold the tiny figurines
of Krishna and Radhika
in my palm as a reminder of us.

They bear the warmth
of your hand when you held mine
and my lips
still remember your kisses.

Like Krishna's flute, spring breeze
whispers your poetry to me
and March rain
waters the tulips in my heart.

Golden moon caresses the seas
that separate us
as the waves of your passion
rock me to sleep.

And I know
that distance is only imaginary
when souls are intertwined.

Elegia as Radhika

Vrindavan - A town in India where, according to Hindu mythology, Lord Krishna and his supreme beloved, Radhika wrote tales of their immortal love

Gopis - Cow-herding maidens

Sunset kiss (Collaboration by Elegia and RJ Kram)

summer sunset
blows rosy kisses
to the still river

*this cherry sky
is a blossom
on the Hudson*

tiny ripples of dusk
tap at our feet

we sit
under the lantern
watching the Tappan Zee
ignite
like a Christmas pine
*as the sun slowly sinks
behind Hook Mountain*

*our tiki flame flutters
in fickle wind*

dark circles
under your eyes
remind of the years
and loves
lost

the bitterness
of divorce

*time has combed
its ragged fingers
through your hair
and hung
every pain
from your cheeks*

but tonight
is our paradise

the taste of your lips
is familiar
like home
and your eyes
are ever young

*we still have
our youthful grins*

*and our sunsets
in Piermont
are countless
as the stars
that follow*

Elegia and RJ Kram (his portion is in Ital)

Becki Friend

Full Circle

I'm Rebecca Friend and I have many nicknames - Becki, Bec, Mom, Grandma and a few I shall refrain from mentioning - but I'm a Friend to all. As a thirty-year social worker fighting child abuse, my name proved a fitting one. I am also a bleeding-heart liberal and a hardcore hippie; I wove flowers in my hair.

I have embraced literature and writing from childhood, my vision of a career in journalism bolstered by selection as college newspaper editor, but unexpected motherhood created income urgency. When I graduated from college, I pursued employment month after month.

One starving, sunny morning I received offers of two positions: a reporter with the local newspaper and a social worker with the county. The county paid fifty dollars more a month.

I became a social worker.

Two more children, a full-time job and graduate school pushed writing aside, but after my recent retirement I stumbled upon AP and discovered a wonderful world of poet friends. I feel as if I've come full circle, returning to writing and my new aphrodisiac... poetry.

I'm also a traveling vagabond, an amateur photographer and a former dancer still dancing, but mostly prancing and playing with grandchildren. If there is one thing I crave more than writing poetry it is music. It has saved me on many occasions. But that is another story.

The Dancer

Sand saturated
by waves
is firm beneath
her bare feet,
like the stage of
polished hardwood
in the abandoned theater
of her adolescence.

A beach towel
hugs slender hips,
purple lotus blossoms
and pink flamingos
flipping in the breeze,

make-shift substitute
for a ballet skirt
of white tulle and
silver gauze.

Using a distant sailboat
as her spot,
the dancer performs
one fouetté turn
in a whirlwind of alabaster hair
before her stamina stalls.

She recalls an encore
performance

of ten dizzying spins,
singing violins and
a standing ovation;

facing the ocean, she curtsies
and bathes in the surf's applause.

Becki Friend

Cutting on the Bias

Folds of chambray
fall across her knees
in liquid-soft layers;
cool and flowing cascades
of blue broadcloth.

With closer look,
a fine-spun grain
materializes;
an arcane, criss-cross stitch
bewitching me.

Her spidery fingers
stroke white weft, blue warp;
crinkled skin
smoothing
a seamless surface.

She pulls a silk thread
between wilted lips
and pierces the needle's eye
in one try, whispering
to herself.

Leaning near, I hear
her words of
ancestral advice:

"Cut on the bias,
to supply us more stretch."

Dedicated to my grandmother, who left this earth many years ago

Becki Friend

Shell Lovers

Trolling the seashore for shells,
we search in silence, knowing
the chill of winter warns us.
This will be the final stroll
until the wind shifts
back to spring breezes.

The water rushing through bare
toes is warmer than the air,
but not for long.

Perfect pink and gray scallop
tumbles to shore,
pausing.
I snatch it up, just ahead
of the ebbing wave,
and add it to the
cozy collection
in my crowded,
wet blue jean pocket;

sandy gems for a glass jar,
keepsakes of walks as countless
as the seashells.

Becki Friend

Blue Raven

Ann Coberley describes herself as a soul divided. She was born and raised in the Texas Panhandle, but moved to New York City as a young adult. She spent 30 years in the city, attending college and graduate school and raising a family. Now returned to Texas, her poetry draws on both the images and landscapes of west Texas, and her history in New York City. Her writing is also influenced by time spent in Italy - 2 years as a resident in Ferrara.

Ann is a wife, mother, and grandmother, a professor of anthropology, a pianist, a reader, a yogi, a meditator, a spiritual seeker, and a writer. She has published two books of poetry about Palo Duro Canyon in Texas, and is currently working on a book of poetry about Texas called "Places of the Heart."

Venice

My gondola
skims through inky waters
of the Venetian lagoon

slipping past the pink lamps
of Piazza San Marco

an ebony black vessel
sleek and polished
dappled with silver moonlight.

Cradled in its bed
of silken cushions
I surrender to the motion
of the waves

to captivating visions
of another time
and thoughts of bygone lives

as we glide silently
through pearls of light
that drop from ancient windows
and drift in the current below.

Blue Raven

Caffè Reggio

Warm light
seeps from foggy windows,
and raindrops splatter
off deserted outdoor tables

while we, snug inside,
take refuge from the weather,
finding comfort
in the hiss of steaming milk
and the aroma of cappuccino.

Dark walls, aged for a century,
are covered with gilded mirrors
and faded landscapes
in antique ornate frames.

Wobbly marble tables
and cushioned banquettes
tuck into dim corners,
air thick with candle wax
and good intentions.

But books and laptops lie idle
as the door wheezes
and friends slip in or out,
always finding time for this place
on a New York afternoon.

Blue Raven

On Horseback

Riding
through a yellow sunrise

across fields
painted by nature
with such passion

that only one
without a soul
would be unmoved

I mourn
what this gilded landscape
meant to the Comanche

filled with buffalo
and undivided
by fences.

Blue Raven

Danna Hobart

Danna Hobart lives in California where she is a full time writer. Her poetry has been published in journals such as Events Quarterly, Zygote in my Coffee, Ink Pot, Problem Child, and Cadenza, and in anthologies Ink Angels, Feeling is First, The Dream Book of Dreams, and others.

Vacancy

It was the perfect night
for a ride in your old, dented-up Chevy,
until you found a train to race.
Sound of its whistle
blew straight through me
as you drove between the crossing gates.

My heart quivered
like the speedometer needle
and your lips were hotter
than your 454 manifold.

The city seemed lonely
looking down from Bear Hill at night.
You told me all your fast ambitions
while drinking a fifth of Jack.
I watched the signal at Cross and Maine

turn from red to green,
and back to red,
avoiding your eyes,
but the moonlight was powdered sugar on my skin
and you were determined to taste it.

Not even the darkness was perfect.
I opened my eyes to the
red neon VACANCY sign
flashing across my face,
while you squeezed my hips and groaned.

Morning sun melted between us
I watched your eyes
in reckless R.E.M. and knew
I'd never share your dreams.

Danna Hobart

Wilted

He found me
a wild rose
on the roadside
stretching toward the sun.

He was a clinging vine;
transplanted himself into my world.
Soon we were tangled together
around a picket fence dream.

We couldn't afford to paint that fence white
even with me working two jobs;
it stayed that gray shade
of weathered wood.

Who needs fresh paint anyway?
He had his cigarettes,
I had my kaleidoscope,
and we read Xaviera Hollander together.

After the children were born
he acted like the world was a slot machine
and it was somehow my fault
it didn't come up all cherries.

I made lots of
lemonade from all those
lemons he brought home
but he would only drink gourmet coffee.

I think of him often now,
and sharply,
like when I pretend his head
is the butter bean I'm snapping.

With an old song though
memory softens and
soon I need both hands
just to hold my heart together.

I know what it means
to give someone your youth.
Twenty-one years of my life
washed away, roots left exposed.

Just tell me please,
how does a flower on the roadside
catch someone's eye
when it's already begun to wilt?

Xaviera Hollander is the author of "The Happy Hooker"
It's basically a guide to great sex

Danna Hobart

Summer Nights

A poem bubbles in me,
peroxide on an open wound;
I smother in the humidity
of summer dreams gone limp
as my sun-bleached hair.

Childhood summers melt together
like crayons left in the yard.

When I was eleven,
summer nights were hide-n-seek
and sneaking into the garage
with a boy four years older than me.

The warmth of his hands
was like the first taste of
grapefruit sprinkled with sugar
but then it all goes sour.

Summer tears burn
worse than bare feet
on hot asphalt.

Now the nights are sticky
too sticky even to fuck,
so we lie, nude
barely touching
aching for relief.

Longing vibrates from deep inside;
the reedy resonance of a Native flute.
There is beauty in desire,
and in reaching for each other
in tepid minutes before sunrise.

On the front porch
cigarette smoke curls.
June Bugs cling to the screen door
and hiss when it slams.
They remind us how to laugh,
as Perseid showers us with new dreams.

Danna Hobart

Dave Kavanagh

Dave Kavanagh: Circa 1964, so a classic for the purpose of classification.

I grew up in a fishing and farming village in the county of Dublin, an adopted son of a family of farmers and fishermen and one dragon that loomed large over all of our lives.
I started writing as a child. I have ADHD and Dyslexia but I was unaware that these conditions precluded me from sharing my insanity so I kept writing for the joy of it.

I hate punctuation (,.!) Little marks on paper that stand in the way of creativity and as a dyslexic I do better without the extra confusion that the rest of humanity need to see the sense in what I write.

I write every day, on paper, on a screen or on the side of dusty delivery vans. I seldom edit until readers' eyes bleed which makes me a little difficult to love. I ignore the chill that often issues from the shoulders and mouths/pens of readers who reel drunkenly from the prose of my illiterate soul.

I am semiretired; I ran a multinational transport business for many years and farmed horses most of my life.

I am now a full time Dad to Adam, almost 17 years old also ADHD and our foster daughter, Rou, who has cerebral palsy but is in my eyes perfect in every way. I have been dancing for thirty five years; childhood sweethearts who never grew out of it.

I have been published quite a bit; poetry, articles and short stories. My first novella will be published shortly (Edits and re-writes allowing). I am working on being published some more, just have to focus on the darn punctuation. My major inspiration comes from diverse strands and threads, whatever tips me on the shoulder, makes me smile, frown, wonder. Genres are for Hollywood, poetry is the story of humanity.

I have had three separate incarnations with IPC, each an education. Last time around I enjoyed the camaraderie of a close knit club of talented poets. I left on that occasion (with a promise to return) to keep a promise to a friend in another group. But now with my commitments fulfilled I am back to write with IPC for the foreseeable future. There are so many wonderful writers at IPC that it would be difficult to pick favorites. Elegia, Blue Raven, Monarch, RK Kram, Becki, Rob Gannon, Bobbie: these are all poets who have inspired me and have encouraged me. Thank you guys!

I am contactable at: www.dave-kavanagh.com

The hardness of geometry (Gold)

Painting the brilliance of sky, my core touching the softness of elder bark in a frantic, static shock world of arc bright white; the wind up here is sharp and pungent, redolent of hops and burnt grain and diesel fumes. My tongue craves surf and salt and the tang of marsh and mud, my nose, the clean stink of razor fish and clams. Mouth tasting in anticipation, chowder and pan fried mackerel.

I am blinded by reflections, glass bouncing a million tiny suns in a billion shattered directions. Men sitting on lunchtime pales and struts; rivet herders, city fellows that sing songs of Philadelphia streets and fast cars, scarlet molls and gangster rappers. Nothing here of sheep on green banks or black and white wisps chasing whistles and fleece back to cirrus framed barns or the silence of my land.

The lemon blue of the dollar clashes with the hardness of geometry, uprights blinding sight of rivers and lakes. The world seen through a matrix of welders' art, rivet guns and bolts as wide as Mary's waist.

Men up here walk on the edge of nothing, whistling suicide as they ride girders through swaths and slashes of turquoise sky.

The metal road heaves and all I feel beneath my feet is the song of deck boards. And a prayer whispering home, calling exiles back to the quietness of a lover's arms.

Dave Kavanagh

Snow in Dublin City

It tumbled and drifted in harmony
with the bells at Christ Church,
the stroke of eight o'clock echoing
across the spire and copper domes.

The river a black ribbon
cutting a route home in fast failing
light,

The city scarred,
sharp and hard, angular,
perpendicular.
All then caressed and soothed
into pristine whiteness
by a gentle hand
A dressing wrapped tight on all the harm.

Traffic fell silent, steam rose
from taxi ranks,
the sound of a shout
shocking,
carried quickly over rooftops.

Feet shuffle in northern dust,
grey and black of streets
disguised in coats of polar fleece.

On railings needles steal the glow
of coal black street lamps
and cast it back in winter shades
of blue and purple, arctic cold,
and silver shattered beams that
pirouette in blurry-eyed crystal visions.

A bus by the toll bridge
spinning its wheels on a carpet,
churned to muck and blood.
A groom plunging against
the mound of a virgin bride.

Traffic begins to move,
cautiously first in the novelty
of gliding, sliding softly
until a mountain of slush
is ridged into lanes,
holding silver, blue and green
streaks in place.

The white gives way to blood gored
from a broken promise.
Waste piled high in dirty shades of
decay.

Starlight returned to a clearing sky,
Mars exploding from a sheet of
frozen black,
larger for his absence.

Only window ledges
and slated roofs still wear evidence
of a miracle,
an hour of pure white silence
in a city restless in its exuberance.

Dave Kavanagh

Rocket Ships & Shooting Stars

I have camped too long
here among rocket ship
   & shooting stars
   In the long lines of shade
thrown by old and gnarled
fig trees.

Here where light pools
like amber oil
and twilight is a blink

   Or less.

   I know the sweetest voice
and loudest silent sigh
   Vibrations of heated desert
breezes.
   I hum my muse to sleep with
the song of shifting sands.

   Now is the time
to spread angel wings
and glide along the silver arc

Time to pack my music box
and my cheap magic tricks,
to stow my opium pipe,
dig up my crimson fire bricks.

To read the future
on faded vellum charts
purchased from
a blue eyed, nomad child.
   Align blue horizon with rising stars,
and the scarlet tip of Mars

Alone, to walk the course
of long dry river beds.
   To divine water from an arid sky
walk the high path
of once rippling waves.

And go,
where ancient seas still flow
in desert dreams.

   To navigate by peaks and dips,
sail on flatulent four
legged ships,
to a new oasis.

And camp again
content,
under the shade of ancient palms.

Dave Kavanagh

Ellafonte

A poet and composer in New York City, Simon Brown enjoys sleeping in on Sundays and cooking with fresh turmeric. He's currently pursuing a Master's in Music from Brooklyn College, where he seems to regularly meet his admired composers. He teaches and conducts at the youth orchestra of St. Luke's, went to Westfield State University, and somehow needs more books (arguably).

"The Indelible Poetry Club is important to me because it's a place to instantly find incredible works any time, along with the satisfaction of being among the first in the world to enjoy these poems."

I miss the curves of certain roads

I miss the curves of certain roads
the way tires cling to asphalt
my hands on the textured wheel
putting a CD in the slot
or even a tape;
listening to the whine
of 30-year old magnetized ribbon
being fed through a 20-year old deck.

I go through my old poems:
last year, two years
like pages of old lovers,
remembering who I am
what I was.
I live Merlin-style
through the blurs of stanzas,
binge reading, rooting
for myself to be born
in verse
inverse.

Travel with me:
become obsessed
with not just who I am now
but where I was
ten years ago, arms like vines
around awful relationships.

I miss the curves of certain letters

the way ink stains the page
and, close-inspected, bleeds
like lightning.

My poems are the paths of least resistance
typed without hesitation
rarely edited
and often flammable.

Travel with me on certain roads
feel the curves
and don't be afraid
to take wrong turns:
we'll always end up
back at your house.

Ellafonte

A lash let loose

a lash let loose
it falls and settles
flash of glitter
one lost hairpin
petal dried and settled in the soil
turquoise splash of paint
a rattle from the kettle

tied up journal
flecks of brown
a slender arc of waist
a drop of water creeping down the glass

an orange sky reflected
spark of current from the plug

a hand around a finger
murmurs
smile painted on a toe

another lash
this one is me
I settle next to you

we're dusk and dawn
two hairs that crossed
two husks of protein

we believe

these tiny things can change the air
while universes flux
we are two hairs

Ellafonte

But why am I here, pulling ribbon

but why am I here, pulling ribbon
I suddenly wonder
stumbling around wal-wart

it won't go back in the spool
glittering purple, twisting in the harsh light
beautiful as a woman's waist

there's nothing to take to the cashier
whom I have to walk by
with the guilt of the innocent
written on my thinning lips

the phone in the car says nine missed calls
and the lot's lights start to spin
lot's wife has been calling
begging
for one more glance

but the ribbon wouldn't go back
I left a sparkling purple mess
and I'm dialing now, trying
to unlock the phone
but tears smear the screen
and cars have been leaving
phone shaking
deep breathing
she's screaming
which comes through the little speaker

like some sort of weird music
for avant-garde Mario

I'm laughing now
thinking about the spool
and what fools pull ribbon
for no reason

Ellafonte

Errant Panther

My name is Scott Venus (a.k.a. Errant Panther). I'm an Australian poet with a tendency to write mostly "free verse" poetry, although I have written in several forms (including one of my own creations called "Dasyure") and some lyrics despite an inability to compose the music necessary to accompany them.

I don't like being defined or confined by any particular style; I just try to convey a message or at least provide an enjoyable / interesting read.

My poetry is not necessarily about myself or my experiences, even if they happen to borrow from them or what I've learned through observing others. I believe life's lessons are out there, I am merely giving them a voice.

I have self published 3 collections of my poetry, which are all available through Amazon and other online booksellers, search for the titles "Finding Wisdom in Shadows", "Whisper Something Fragile" and "Breathing Moments".

I am in the process of compiling a manuscript for an as yet untitled 4th collection. Most of my time is occupied being the caretaker of two housemates with varying degrees of disability, so sincere thanks in advance to anyone who chooses to purchase my books, as both these endeavors are done for love not profit.

Of Feathers and Faith (Vignettes)

i.

twist the shades
of scattered petals

let them fall as notes
across forgotten piano keys

staining life
with their own melody

ii.

cascading blooms
piercing memory
obscuring
all sense of what is
and what was

an unintentional nuance
of acceptance

iii.

shards of the self
I thought I knew
pervade deep into this mirror
seemingly taunting
as though it were

an unfinished puzzle
daring me to restore it

into order

iv.

ignited
beneath the breath of hope
all but lost
in a sea of grey

a strange, uneasy urge
to push beyond the void,
seizes control,
sacrificing vanity for liberty

v.

numbness and uncertainty
suddenly ebb amid a tide
of self imposed repression

a timid awakening of spirit
not yet finding faith enough
to take flight

vi.

as the sky dissolves
its partnership
with clouds of angst

new wings unfurl
sensing an air of prosperity
against tentative feathers
seeking to flutter

into the unknown

vii.

finally released
this soul begins a new
and intrepid journey

discovering all
that was once omitted
or ignored
for the sake of pride

viii.

trace the edges
of your own feathers

twist the shades
of tainted petals ...
see where your colours fall

take the leap of faith
into an unknown future
despite a fear of flight
or resign yourself
to clutch the shoulders

of misery
and join the misbegotten

Errant Panther

Take a Chance (Dasyure Form)

A heart tied in knots,
no-one close to hear my cries.
Your gift, crushed by feet, forget-me-nots;
how can I forgive your lies.
Leave, never return.

My trust sacrificed,
ruins you need not concern.
Your toxic love, from my life excised,
I'll be your victim no more.
Love, keeps not the score.

Life's full of subplots,
circumstance often denies.
Why should we accept fate like robots,
seek destiny with fresh eyes,
let passion's flame burn.

New purpose devised,
stale, forgotten dreams now yearn.
Faith and ideals no longer chastised,
freedom your soul can't ignore,
take a chance, explore.

Errant Panther

Kicking Up the Rain

like delicate hands
grasping at receding tendrils
of fading memory

a plaintive heart recoils

dignity sacrificed
at the altar
of a new infatuation

remorseless
despite an irregularity in rhythm

impulses override composure
without any second thought
as to their destructive impact

all that glitters certainly
isn't gold

and the one that stands alone
in the wake of such treachery

wanders aimlessly through puddles
of tears shed upon hollow ground

caressing thoughts of what may have been
whilst kicking up the rain.

Inspired in part by the Bronski Beat song "Kicking up the Rain" and also by thoughts many have in regards to lost love.

Errant Panther

Fragmented Sage

Michael Schepers resides in beautiful Guelph, Ontario, Canada. Mike loves family and so it fit him well when he married young and immediately had children. He has not looked back in thirty five years. In this time he started a landscape gardening business and got more kids. A lot of successes and failure have taken place over this time, all of it quantifiable. Many seasons have also gone by and these too are quantifiable. Mike will say he tries to do just that and wish he started earlier.

It has only been two years since Mike started writing. He joined AP at the suggestion of his brother Albert and has not looked back. Haiku suited him well as they best expressed the different seasons and ironies of life. The break out moment that "allowed" him to experiment with different forms was thanks to fellow poets on this site. (Thank you Dana for that first contest)

Sounds of Silence

litter
in the perfect night
stars

a low dull echo
of muffled grayness
as the leaded line
fathoms the empty
of the barrel

over this a gust
too gauging depth
drawing out the vacuous
that the plumb line
has somehow missed

the widow smiles
and draws out one cup
she lights again the lamp
that dances and flickers
to the rhythm of the dark

she sits waiting
for a kind interlude
soft steps in gravel
muffled creak of stoop
and the slosh of an amphora

it was yesterday

her barrel was drained
the cost of perfect darkness
carved out of a cave
her tomb purchased

these tones and sepia
that inspire the dirge
drawn from nothing's teat
thick black notes
that sound of silence

the bat sees
in the spectrum
of sonar

FragmentedSage

Season of Joy

scarred and rough limbs
protrude from under raw hemp
I clear dirty socks from bed
and clip the old girl's nails
the winter rose stirs

One thing I love about the garden is that the plants never know the seasons. They awake in the spring with bed head but have no mirror to tell them how they should feel. Plants do not write of that gooey sappy blood coursing through their cambium. They do not blog about having to carry a bud to full term; or strut when it blooms. There is nothing in plant lore about the bugs and lost blooms or the feel of the cold wind over supple leaves. There are no battle hymns sung about the meadow wars and no lost letters found about littered seed pods. If we humans were like nature we would sing the same song each morning, like the birds, and not write this Haibun to talk about it. If plants crushed their neighbor in scalding water each morning while considering their options for the day they would still sow the same seed.

the stinging nettle
and the rose
plant joy

FragmentedSage

My Walker

The leaf rolled beside her,
unshod and long past supple.
It chattered along with clicked skips
and a breezy gait;
finally matching her pace.

It was the leaf's monologue
that drew my eye to her.
She was stealth.
There was no spring in her step;
no season at all.
No drooped fall shoulders
or swagger of spring.
Nothing sultry.

It was not the leaf,
the push of traffic
or pulse of street lights
that paced her
though they all kept up.

I looked long
pondering tuned instruments,
dressage
and pebbles in shoes.
I wanted to learn her tune.
To hear the way
waves lapped her core.
To hear the beat

of this solo drummer
and feel the pull of the oars
through her sinew.
I wanted to watch her prow
crest and fall
generating this wake
that pulled along that leaf.

Her father would be proud
and I did beam.

FragmentedSage

HuesFac3

Photo credit:
http://wallpapersafari.com/w/EqQkCv/

Diamonds

And now the trickles ripple rifting
through hues of the sky—confetti!
The words of my mouth are paintings;
a projected splash all over—frantics!
Whether they drag down God's face
blaze out streamlights—candlelights
pin a billion sunrises into a stiffened day.
How over-good—worthless crystallites?

When they fall on mangrove skies;
borrowed zephyrs compress—upsize;
explode into sands of mustard seeds—ripe!
Germinate tons of thorns—stars—torn
prickles—squeals—resounds—muted cries;
the act of the hands, when they try and try
to seal the width and pit of the mouth—'unrise'
head's cap size—safeguard the crown—discrown.

How over-good—worthless crystallites?
The River births—your River mouth—'silverlites'
the tributaries—tributes—waterfalls —silver bird—
the screeching lines—over-stretched verse;
voice box machines—the echoes—out loud;
on the stainless-steel wall—a still pass
into dwindling star flaps—eyes lashed
How over good, all these worthless crystallites?

HuesFac3

Splash

Splash all over me;
your mighty-mini fervor—
the weight of your fluorescence;
lights up the crescents
with a zillion butterflies.

Splash on the wall;
a projection of your smile—
your Thirty-Two crystal beads;
alleviate the night,
sustain morning light.

Splash in the sky;
today's golden glow—
your cat eyes reflect the sun;
illuminate the day,
at night the Milky Way.

Splash in the night;
The Heaven's on Earth—
all hovering stars with a wink;
a night of hues,
for me and you.

HuesFac3

Wait-rose

Wait-rose, waits, and waits
on the water-washed shore
to greet the pebbles
with its mind's murmurs;
yelp muted groans and roars

With a slick of teardrop
that could still sail
in silence on the cheeks
highway down the shallows
of the blue-hued pebbles

its arrival splats and a splash
of crystal blood droplets
erupt the quiet falls
with a slam and mind-crash;
stables turn sables and fumbles

and just like the blackout
in a silver moon's day night
when the mighty rushes pass
with a trample on the brain
and all its fragile membranes

Wait-rose, waits, and waits
and the waterfall bends
its head to salute the mirrored

floor opening the Milky Way
into underlaid 'dreamstars'

HuesFac3

Irene Clasper

Alka Rao is a young poetess from India who writes under the pen name Irene Clasper. She has long witnessed the power of ink, initially through masters and later, her own poetry and in the long run wishes that her works leave behind a luminous trace larger than her own existence.

She smelled like a cyclone [Vignettes]

i.

The rhythmic sweeps of wind that swooshed beside her created a symmetry of rhapsody. Every depression of her wooden stiletto in the mud accentuated the hiatus between her two heartbeats. Her stride down the unevenly forged road was periodically shortened by the pull of desperate thoughts that outweighed her mass. As she crushed autumn leaves beneath her odium, ignominy rose like rouge in her cheeks.
The frequency with which her past revisited her
had left her a mortal
of deliquescent soul

and febrile bark

ii.

packing her coat
with cerebral repulsion;
she left the calculation
of good and evil to the
puffs of breeze

her agitation seemed to
force the lustrous moon
to orbit closer to the earth
with greater dynamism

iii.

the leaden basilica
that hovered above
the landscape
had cloudy strands
that embroidered
lunar illustrations

insomniac constellations
mocked at the timid
figure that wriggled beneath;

as they gradually traveled
their course to gain
a complete view
of her handicapped sanity

iv.

She dropped her guilt
capsuled in sequins of her blouse
shredding the shadows of louse
as the sedimented silt

oomph leaving her shell
through tips of her displaced hairs
traversing with the night as pairs
leaving her as a mute rebel!

v.

the autumn of her soul
gradually hovered in
depression of ignominy

mute agitation capsuled
in odium
beneath shadows of sanity

Irene Clasper

Whimsicalities of ordinary on a Stranger

i. Dawn sleeved ingenuity

Sun-burnt trees strolling
with a stranger of
Prunella cloaked moderns
gauging the strength of cemented tiles
to fill the intermediate gaps left from insomniac footprints
with his own pigmented dreams
hoping these serve milestones to his rainbow

with the last of the lanterns turned down
a diabolical tale treaded into busy streets
mimicking humanity.

ii. Singed noon blues

Peering out into reality
through a clean conscience
and rusted iron window bars
painting an imaginary tree
of crimson leaves and over-grown stem
which split light into monochromatic beams
that reach out into fairy tales
and grasp the chord that vibrates
with an intensity similar
to his broken harmonica

A resonance of imbalanced mentality!

iii. Retrospective dusk of triviality

Every street lamp summarizing
their day's observations
of ginger red hairs to pimpled souls
into a spherical sulphur pool
on the well-beaten roads
where insights swim and dissipate
absorbing passing dementia
of varying lunatic frequencies

The stranger now tracing back
his morning symphonies
sending twilight in search of
rooted equilibrium that lies tousled
and brooding amidst hands of shadowed sand clocks

ticking off ingenious seconds to singed trivialities!

Irene Clasper

Together we are a rainbow in brume's attic

They asked me what it was to be with you.

My words implacably scratched my taste buds
    not wanting to leave
        fearing they might mistakenly
            drop one of your vowels

I offered a lame one.

' If you ever know

what is to have dusk cracking on your lips
being vulnerable to the imperfections around
yet refracting them at the speed of light
see them perish like a smoked cigarette
and finally curl down
settle on your ambient memories
then you know what I mean'

I didn't tell them the truth.

' When metaphors start stripping the sun
evolving into rispettos that crystallize in my
vena cava leaving behind the caffeine like
addictive felicity loose and unsecured in my
breath and the horizon finally sweats crashing
into the ocean below.

        You are that poem. '

Irene Clasper

James C. Allen

Allen, James C.
Georgia, USA

Award-winning writer of modern poetry going back to the nineteen seventies. My first book, "Saying Goodbye to Rue" published September 2014 by Shoestring Book Publishers is available from Amazon.com, Barnes and Noble, and Lulu.

I am a three-time winner of the prestigious Dr. Bruce Dawe O.A. prize, first for the poem, "The Final Viewing of the Tulips" published in Prism Contemporary International Poetry Anthology, Editor Ron Wiseman, 2015.

In addition, I was selected Prism Anthology Laureate, June 2015.

Recent Awards:

Winner: The Eye of the Poet Competition for poem, "Across the Universe" – December 2014
Printed in Prism Contemporary International Poetry Anthology – Editor Ron Wiseman, Australia – Available from Lulu Independent Publishers

Winner: Dr. Bruce Dawe Prize for poem, "The Pines, New York circa 1985" – April 2016
Winner: W.H. Auden Prize for poem, "Diagnosis" – April 2016
Both Appear in Prism Contemporary International Poetry Anthology – Editor Ron Wiseman, Australia and Jo Elle, Belgium – April 2016, Prism #19 – Available from Lulu Independent Publishers

Winner: Sylvia Plath Memorial Prize for poem, "Winter Becomes Electra" – June 2016
Winner: Clive James Prize for poem, "Tennessee" – June 2016
Winner: Dr. Bruce Dawe OA Prize for poem, "Light Years of An Exceptional Boy" – June 2016
Prism #20 Available from Lulu Independent Publishers

Affiliations/Memberships

Life Member: Allpoetry.com
Fellow: Prism Group
Fellow: International Poetics Foundation
Co-Editor: International Poetry Fellowship Anthology, "Pepperoni Pizza" – December 2016.

Why I Love Bobby Sharp

We met under unusual circumstances,
me still mourning
my lifetime companion,
yet surprisingly not alarmed.

There exists a spiritual axiom;
when a person of significance
is taken, another arrives.

Just as all who have become friends,
he held magic enough
to provide healing for the broken.

In that first moment after he sang,
any possibility I had been misdirected
vanished like haze from an illumined
pond.

And then the confirmation,
knitting of bones I had thought
would never again be able to
sustain the weight of my loss.

If fortunate,
we are introduced to a Bobby
who will plug emptiness
until we heal
with strength derived
from internal bandages.

Before, do not be shocked,
this man of youth
tentative in voice,
will arrive to provide
hope only the hopeless
can comprehend.

James Allen

In Romania Tonight

The quake near Bucharest 6.1 on the Richter;
my closest friend is there.
I reach him by Skype I can see he is alive
though his neighbor is in shock;
the conversation ends abruptly
he must help the ill.

No big deal, no deaths reported
but on the top of the glass table
where the monitor sits, my handprints
in beads of sweat.

Despite all my precautions
my refusals to leave the house
after my lover died,
this little bastard has
gotten past my defenses.

I've sinned against myself,
broken my oath to remain
numb forever,
to make no room to care
for another human,
yet here it is inside of me

and on the table as well.

James Allen

Resuscitation of the Blue Boy

Sunday when my lover died,
the right side of the chandelier
went dark all at once.

I took it as a sign,
realized there would be
a permanent absence,
seven ruined filaments
flickering a final time
before darkness loomed
forever.

I grew old, dull as
neglected brass,
that three tiered
monstrosity hanging
above the table
like a giant failed fuse.

I never thought again of love
just saw our past in Fred,
my darling imitation.

One day I made him cry
just before a show,
he knew what he had done
raised me from a tomb,

kissed me like a soldier
saluting recollection

of days that swam in light.

Inspired by the kindness of my friend, Fred

James Allen

Linda Marshall

A proud Romani poet!

Linda Marshall is a Romany gypsy who is passionate about defending the rights of her people. She lives in England though she has also lived and worked in Turkey and Saudi Arabia. She is married with two children, a boy and a girl.

Her poetry is about her people, about nature (which she adores), about political and social issues that engage her (not simply Romany ones) and about her Christian faith.

She writes in a variety of styles and loves rhyme and free verse equally. She also translates the work of poets she admires, mainly from the German or Romanes though she has done a few French, Russian and Turkish translations.

The Porajmos

'Porajmos' is a Romanes word meaning 'the devouring,' is the term used by the Romani people to refer to the gypsy holocaust under the Nazis. Nearly a million died because of their race. (On a personal note, my Uncle Jaime was a porajmos survivor who had his parents, brother and sister murdered in Auschwitz. This poem was written following a visit there.)

I, a stranger, walk the trail of tears
shared by my race.
Like them, I carry an alien face.
Even after all these years
our deaths remain unmourned, ignored.
The crowd of tourists thronging round
at Auschwitz now seems almost bored.
With so much horror in the TV news
can tears of pity for the past be found?

I, trembling, try to take stock
of thirteen years of madness and cruel death:
Auschwitz, Chelmno, Bialystok;
I catch my quivering breath.

Here and now, in this dreadful place
I stand alone,
the only representative of my race
and hear the drone
of others thinking 'only my death matters.'

They should remember what the poet Donne said:
'Each man's death diminishes me.' Idle chatter
from increasingly bored tourists fills my head
and I escape to a much earlier time,
to relive in myself the vicious crime.

I am alone and frightened as I stand
watching the familiar uniform
of the SS driving us from our land,
and then, like a huge swarm
of stinging wasps, on to the train they led us,
And made us promises of work and homes,
And even dignity. Oh, how they bled us!
Our blood soon reddened the mighty ocean's foam.

I am a gypsy girl today,
I, waiting for the train to take me
Into the darkness where they soon will make me
Abandon earth forever. I must pay,
I and my people, for what they call the crime
Of being homeless, wandering the road,
Passing our time
In our hand-painted vardos, with our load
Of kipsis and other goods to sell.
For this they sentenced us to hell.

I, a gypsy, out of India, wandering,
I, betrayed, stripped, beaten, raped and slain;
I, who but yesterday was dukkering
The vast of a rakli, slaughtered on the plain.

I am surrounded, cursed and spat upon,
Lied to and about;
My blood is slowly oozing out:
I shall never bear a son.

The heroes in black are raising their fists
And punching and kicking me into the ground;
There is no strength left in my wrists,
Nor any help to be found.

I, naked, dripping with sweat and blood,
Am dragged, too weak to scream, towards the shower;
They do not want to wash me clean of blood
But to destroy me in this evil hour.

And now they bundle me into the room
Which now I know will be my bitter tomb.
The gas pours in; I try to catch my breath,
But there's no cheating this unwelcome death.

Not a bird sings as I pass away,
Not a flower blooms as I am cast aside;
Just yesterday I should have been a bride,
And gladly married miri ro,
Yet here I am and now to hell I go,
Or death at least. Divvel, pray for me now!
I'll soon be fertiliser for the plough.

I am a single voice
Mourning the loss of 800,000 folk
Who, under the bitter yoke

Of tyranny, were slain.
We had no choice;
Death was the only way to end our pain.

Out of the thousands who died
Mine is only a single cry
For the old and the young,
The women and men,
Who were led out to die
Again and again:
I am only their voice.

Here, in Auschwitz, Chelmno, Bialystok,
I watch the crowds of tourists flock.
The holocaust deniers spin their lies;
The special pleaders will not grant our place
Beside their own. 'Gypsies are not a race,'
Or so they, lying, say, and with insincere sighs
Try to round down the numbers of our dead,
And almost blame us. Oh, the bitter bread
We eat even today! The evil names
They call us as they try to bring us shame!
Yes, I'm a gippo, pikey, call me what you will:
Love always conquers hate, and always will.

The porajmos - the genocide of Europe's gypsies - is one of the darkest hours in the history of the continent and certainly the darkest in the history of my people. My poem attempts to relive the horror of that time. I wrote it following a visit to Auschwitz where my uncle - a porajmos survivor - lost his parents, brother and sister.

I have used a few Romani expressions in the poem. 'Vardos' are the old-fashioned wooden gypsy caravans; 'kipsis' are baskets'; 'dukkering the vast' means reading the hand or reading the palm; 'rakli' is a non-gypsy woman; Divvel is one of our names for God - it's from a Sanscrit root similar to Zeus and has nothing at all to do with the Devil; 'miro ro' means my husband or my man.

Auschwitz, Chelmno and Bialystock were three of the camps where our people suffered and died. My uncle was in Auschwitz.

Linda Marshall

Embracing Autumn

our youth flees as the seasons do;
as the leaves fall from the trees
so too we age

shards of summer remain,
but the mushy jetsam
is trodden underfoot, unnoticed

all the rich plumage of summer
abandoned on the sodden earth,
a child's now unwanted toy

the branches of trees
bend in the inclement wind
and try to resist his mating cries

they wait in their turn
for the coming time when the wind will shake
like a cocktail from the sky the first snowflake

the rocks, the little stream
flowing through the wood
will be decked out in frost and crystals of ice

summer is gaudy, a fashion parade
of garish colour;
autumn is sober, burnishing life in russet and brown

when the light around fades
the sky sheds its colour,
trees become shadows in the wood

it is not yet the barrenness of winter
but the mellow ripeness of too rich fruit
that autumn brings

so we embrace you, autumn;
promise that though we too perish and change
we will return, endure

Linda Marshall

For the risen Christ

The sky shut its eyes in shame, the ground beneath
Heaved up its sighs; then all was still at last,

Only the wailing of the watching women
Breaking the awed silence.

Later, in a tomb Christ was laid
in a winding-sheet of white,
And a heavy stone rolled before
The entrance to the tomb

Three days passed, and the earth shook again,
The wind swung violently and tore the air
And the stone rolled away from His burial place,
And all around was filled with sudden light

And Mary, come to weep and to anoint His body,
Found the sight that met her gaze
Like dew on a parched flower at early light,
And Mary saw the living hands and feet
And felt as stunned and awed as if the stars
Had been uprooted from the sky
And hurled down to the bottom of the ocean.

Stilled the crimson blood
That flowed once, yet again
He breathes, He speaks

And out of that day we live,
Our wounds, our sins, healed by His sacrifice.

Through His atonement,
our at-one-ment.

Linda Marshall

Mark Andrew James Terry

Hi. Thank you for reading my poems. I'm Mark Andrew James Terry. I have lived in Orlando, Florida my entire life, having roots that extend generations here. My decades as a commercial artist and marketing executive have been constantly framed by aesthetics. An active arts advocate, I find that poetry is the perfect synthesis of a lifetime expressing myself with painting, music and photography. I see the rhythm of music, the vivid imagery of photography and the free emotional expression of painting as the foundation of my poems. I write in form and in free verse about moments, loves, history, the environment and social injustice. You can read more of my poems on **AllPoerty.com**.

Dreaming Springing

Legendary Airie Fairy,
whisper color on my lawn;
winging, carry pools that vary —
hues from heaven-painted dawn.

Fragile feathers brush the heathers,
blushing every thicket's throng;
tint with fuchsia, how it tethers
even to the rose's prong.

After touring effervescence,
fly again this Bre-hyll view;
rain your tearing iridescence,
glisten leaves with mystic dew.

As your fervor blossom's arbor
rioting my winter's glen,
mark it as a verdant harbor,
tell your friends and come again.

Mark Andrew James Terry

The Econ's Fishin' Hole

Sugar-white sand is edged by ocher grasses
where softly dappled shadows transform
under warm-gray tangled moss
clinging to wet-kneed cypress.

Regally rising, they clutch cumulous clouds
calmly lingering in an intensely cerulean-infused sky
diminished by far-away white.

There is no horizon's view,
only the ancient creek.

Tannin water sifts through cattails,
its coca-cola hues deepening in whorls
and swirls, where eddies churn crevasses
and sunfish teem in schools.

Lily pads float their leafy hearts,
green with tapered stems diving,
while buds open alizarine crimson to pink fingers.

The morning's dense humidity fades
distant burnt-umber forest pines'
true green to dark needles,
and fanning palmettos of dusty green
grip at the creek's edge framing the shore.

There, a snowy egret's inverted image
is broken by light-wind ripples

across the sky's reflection and
a catfish tail slaps the surface.

All is as it always was on the Econlochatchee.

The Econlochatchee flows north to meet the St. John's River through Central Florida scrub pines and a childhood fishing hole.

Mark Andrew James Terry

Morning Wok Scramble

My wooden spoon
cajoles flavors, textures:
rice vermicelli,
shitake mushrooms,
grated ginger root,
their aromatics waltzing
diced garlic cloves
as a prized Purple Onion
simmers with Ella's jazz,
anticipating the beat
of six bantam eggs
and a splash of sake.

Mark Andrew James Terry

MJ Donnelly

*Weary-Eyed,
I Smile and Rise*

Michael J. Donnelly, aka (MJ Donnelly) is a married, fifty-something male, born and raised in Iowa, now living in Alaska. He does have some college education in the form of a few semester hours of technical and creative writing obtained as an Army Non-Commissioned Officer years ago. Michael has always enjoyed writing and has concentrated more on poetry, free verse and rhyme in the past several years as a gold member of AllPoetry.com.

He is published in a few poetic compilations through "The Winklings," a group of ambitious AP poets. Now also a member of the group, "Indelible Poetry Club," he continues to hone his skills gleaning and sharing with many talented writers. Michael's desire is to publish his own books of poetry after retirement as a Federal Law Enforcement

Professional. Michael's favorite poets are; Samuel Beckett, W.B. Yeats, Seamus Heaney, and C.S. Lewis.

Michael writes because his spirit needs it, like an addict craving drugs, like a drunkard with the shakes, he must have his fill! The ideas flitter around in his mind as myriads of glowing butterflies at midnight. At times, he writhes in agony till the morning breaks. Weary eyed he smiles and rises, giving thanks for another day reaching for his journal to jot down the cryptic lexes and visions his muse so frantically shared. He is a writer, a muse-driven steaming locomotive barreling down the tracks at one hundred miles an hour, and a humble word-hungry sage, scratching his heart's messages on the shores of life, hoping someone will read them before time washes them away.

Three Fingers of Jameson Gold Reserve, Neat

Sullivan's bar is a swanky place with polished oak, brass furnishings and a live jazz band to set a sophisticated mood.

The night I retire, I'll swagger in silver haired, dressed in Joseph Abboud's best with wingtips and a hint of expensive cologne, and tell the waitress, "Three fingers of Jameson gold reserve, neat, golden whiskey for a golden day", and I'll smile like Sam Elliott, with soulful eyes.

I suppose she'll enquire what I'm celebrating and I'll tell her, "The end of a long career that a lot of young men don't complete."

I suspect she'll say, "Oh, and what would that be?" and I'll explain, "A profession of thankless service, heart pounding exhilaration with soul-wrenching pain you see, I wore many hats, I was a peacekeeper, a sheep dog protecting the flock from ravenous wolves, a fatherly figure with no children of my own, a counselor, spiritual guru of sorts, a modern-day paladin in blue who battled selflessly and wept in silence, you see, I was a cop."

I will cherish the look on her face; I will sigh like I've never sighed before knowing I have sacrificed, bled, screamed and fought through many anguished trials and lived.

I will sip that whiskey and may even shed a few tears as the tender, human side of me reflects listening to soothing jazz.

MJ Donnelly

Ghosts Muse and Count All of Autumn's Crisp Leaves

Mystical wraiths blow their chilled breath at eaves
Reminding us all that summer has passed,
This icy notice into our soul cleaves;
With a certain cruel punishing blast.

Gunmetal bare trees quiver in their wake,
First frost will soon cover all with a gleam,
Crystal grace will blanket flora and lake;
Whispering to all, "Go to sleep and dream."

Children laughing roll in umber and gold,
Specters dance in vortices of dry leaves
Touching each one, round fingers they are scrolled,
A solemn tall pine; bows its head and grieves.

Cold noses find comfort in warm dry sleeves;
Ghosts muse and count all of autumn's crisp leaves.

MJ Donnelly

Shimmering Salvation

The devout grasp
their sterling crucifixes
on bent knees, mouthing
novenas by candlelight,
my shimmering salvation is;
forty-five, nine millimeter
one hundred and twenty-
four grain hollow points.

MJ Donnelly

Monarch

*Butterfly, butterfly,
come to me
coming, coming,
came… uh-oh!*

Hello buds, bees, birds and breasts. Whoops! Beasts, not breasts. I am known by many names: Pea-cock particularly is interesting (for obvious reasons, of course). But I love it most when they sigh, Monarch, even though there are no golden spots on my skin. I like it that way, it sounds aphrodisiac and kingly. Also because it gives me free license to shamelessly pamper flower petals; I am easily lured by rare scents and bulbous butts. Buds, darn, blame it on my youthful taste-buds and extra sensitive palps.

Fluttering in the heart of India, *Dilli*, I seek the elusive spring in narrow nooks of cobblestoned alleys. Sometimes, I find it on short floral skirts of *desi* virgins, at others, on the terrace in young marigolds blooming on the balcony of my neighbor's daughter. The terrace, from where stars appear a little closer and I can speak, intimately, to raingods; monsoon is a magical muse.

On evenings, when the old radio set croons Ghalib's ghazals to a chorus of cooing pigeons, tinkling rickshaw bells and chants from the nearby temple, I spread my poetic wings and carve the naked winds with poetry. And for a while, the entire universe writhes in an orgy, gasping on the cusp of an immaculate orgasm.

(Shhhh, keep it platonic)

It all started many months ago, when a fragrant gust carried me into a divine meadow, where no flower ever wilts and gentle breeze of love and verse sprinkles fresh seeds on fertile soil; **the Indelible Poetry Club.**

In this meadow, I found a new span and color for my wings, blushing flower-buds to sip upon in every season and magnificent songbirds to listen to on lonely nights; and how easily the subtle beats of my fragile poetic soul dissolved in seductive eloquence. It was in this meadow, beneath the folds of an unfurling tulip, I realized that spring, is always only a breath away.

Butterflower

By midnight she is swollen;
a coy bud
wet and full with rain
tilting at the carnal brush of
warm gusts.

She opens
when moonbeams
fall into places where she is bare.

A petal clings to her skin by
flimsy threads of sap
and barely touches
my palps
before it folds back shyly
around tighter layers.

Shamelessly
I push my wings through the edge
of her softest veil.

Aroused by her scent
and occasional quiver I follow
her trickles
blindly
slipping deeper into
the cove
where she hides the
sweeter pools

and her stalk leans helplessly
as I sip
until my flutters become
her unfurling

Monarch

Longing lips

How unjust
that we should yearn
for such trifles as a touch.
We,
whose pulse mirrors
across waters
and hearts ripple in same shivers.
Shame,
that callous stars should shun
the desperate pleas of restless tears.
We,
whose fates would ramify
in same rivers
should our palms align
and each drop of sweat and blood
would blend to yield the perfect red.
Why on earth
should heavens forbid
our skin, carved like twins, to kiss?
When everyday
our words make love
and every breath echoes one tune,
isn't it fair,
oh gods of love
our lonely lips be bound
till death?

Monarch

पुकार

The river cries, half naked, her veil
smeared
by ashes of the callous dead,
sobbing on shoulders of drooping willows
for her lost children; little rivulets
and meadows,
some decaying leaves.

There are no more gods in stones
she washes,
no foliage sheltering her adolescence;
just ghosts rising from pyres
and brick walls
ambushing her flow.

The same petals she watered lie wilted
around coffins of her virginity.
Shamed and embarrassed she wanders
disheveled
seeking a tear from some distant cloud,
begging with stagnant swamps.

No one listens.

Monarch

MusicBox Metaphor

Mia Amélie Robidoux is an earth writer, otherwise known as a geographer. Born in New Mexico, formed in New Zealand, and raised in Wisconsin, Mia has spent her adult life loving and learning in Chicago, then struggling as an anarcha-feminist and a graduate student-worker in Toronto. Next stop: Montréal. As a decade-old Allpoetry.com member and a new addition to the Indelible Poetry Club, Mia cherishes the insight found in the words of her peers. As a poet, she's currently stuck on trauma, on heartbreak, on how the two relate. She searches for home. She finds healing. And love. There is that.

Father

You rarely find a loon alone.
I wonder if you were concerned,
casting out the words I'd known
for years. Downhill the water ferned

its fingers round the only stone
thrown out by you back when I learned
you rarely find a loon alone.
I wonder if you were concerned

that day I came to you, all grown.
You, in your way, forgot years earned
and lost, left the stone unturned
and looked at me as if I'd flown.
You rarely find a loon alone.

MusicBoxMetaphor

The Mud Room

The keys to 7C sit lonely on the hook.
The open tops of heavy boxes
nudge my knees. I push back,
scrape their corners with my shoes.

Last night, these keys ripped
the mouths of unpacked boxes, slicing
through postage seals, severing
return from current address.
My boxes and I sat with parted lips
and spilled the last traces of sea breeze.

I listen to these living rooms,
the crooked stair,
the humming light-switch.
Steps creak the floors
that roof me, and somewhere
on floor 6, a kettle burns
hot as a steamer.

The cat's claws puncture fresh paint,
etching signs of life into the mud room.

And I try too:
scratch fingers over exposed
brick and imagine pummus
under my hands;

scour the dusty residue
of marble tile and sense
your grainy scent of sand dollars;
set the cat's bowl on the floor
and let the waves slip
over the edge;
tap the keys into a sway
of shadows on beige walls
like fish swimming
against the current.

When they still
their eyes, the hooked holes
watch me walk the shores of 7C.

MusicBoxMetaphor

The Following Sea

I wanted to love her
the way the sun pours
into the shore,
the way the dunes sway
to the breeze's tune
so gently,
not like the water

wrapping
pulling
licking

at my knees. How easy
it should have been to love
the sand as she cradled me,
tracing every edge
with her warmth, absorbing
every heave, every

lungful of water

I held on to. Memories—
a time when light
combed my hair and glossed
my smiles,
a time when burning sands
and singing winds would keep me,
a time when all I knew was land;

but how
do I forget

drowning—
the salty taste of weeds,
the swell of ice
in my tight throat,
moonbeams swimming
through reaching fingers,
sinking arms.

How do I
find comfort,

find comfort in air,
how breathing feels—
the tenderness of in,
the freedom of ex.

All I can do is scream
into the sea.

MusicBoxMetaphor

Only Rob

Northern ink!

Rob Ganson (Only Rob) is a poet/activist from the shore of Lake Superior. Rob lives on a tiny poem farm on the edge of the Chequamegon national forest with his wife and a fine setter.

Rob tends to write on themes of nature and the human condition, and is not popular with the extraction industry. He can often be found behind a bullhorn, sign, or light brigade action on the front lines of an environmental fight, or at the state capital, making friends.

Rob has published four volumes of poetry and been included in numerous journals and anthologies. If you see him at an action or a reading, he will be the bearded jester with the wheeze.

Detritus

Do you look at the trees I planted, the flowers,
or see them in my poems,
and know they will die?

Never mind the boxed books, the yellowing
journals, the scraps, fragments
in my favorite nooks.

Never mind the diatribes, shouted into the sky,
scolding a thousand gods
for what they let us do.

Never mind the soft and broken chair, my lair,
my despair at the disrepair
evident in our "civilization."

Never mind my tiny nation, those five green acres,
the ashes in the vegetable garden,
in the waterfall.

Divorce those things; pay no attention to the loons,
the coyotes I sang with,
let my verbose leaves fall.

Look at your river, flowing in the kitchen painting,
let your iris carpet your kingdom
and your own song fill the air.

Pile my detritus at the side of the blacktop with a sign
that reads free, free like him,
but shed no tear, sing no hymn.

None of those things are me, you see, none sacred
when I have died, when I climb
that ladder of smoke into the sky.

Revel in the quiet I kept from you.

Only Rob

Speaking of Water

(Trigger warning - confrontational topic)

Words for water slip through my mouth
like water through my fingers
water that lingers on the earth
for a time then runs South
dancing with mirth over grandfather stones

My children and theirs drink water
not oil from North Dakota, not mercury
from Minnesota not poison from the mines
that eats away with cancer at Appachlian minds
or Michigan's acid and doom

I speak of pipelines at Standing Rock
indigenous heroes standing tall
of open pit disasters in the land of waterfalls
I speak of Monsanto, of Cargill, of
animal factories that no more resemble farms
than I resemble bankers or kings
I scream the names of those
who cause the children harm, raise alarms
with a failing voice and a thunderous bullhorn

I stand beneath the embrace of warm rains
bathing in magic from the sky, and feel pain
for the next seven generations
who will not have clean water,
who will bathe in acid rain, and all for a nation
of potentates who enable the extractors, industry kings

with pipelines, hog factories, poisoned mines
to festoon the fingers of their concubines
with the filthy weight of diamond rings
and bags and vaults filled with monopoly money

Protectors stand at Standing rock, stand
on sacred ground, stand atop the Penokee spine
stand to stop the Menomonee mine
stand in Minnesota, in West by God Virginy
where orange rivers reek with shame
stand in the name of children to come
stand where the Colorado used to roam
stand to protect their water, their homes
but everywhere we stand, the man with the devious plan
buys the politicians, sends mercenaries
soldiers, police to stand against THE PEOPLE

I speak of the Sioux river, the rain that feeds my garden
and me, that feeds Mother Superior, the inland sea
but three miles up the hill, the blasting grounds
fester, with mounds of poisoned earth, jagged metal
where nothing lives but fear, and three miles further
up that hill, Enbridge has a time bomb snake
ready to burst forth with a lake of oil, and then
the Chequamegon will be awash in death

The pipeline WILL leak; it isn't a question of if but when

I ask tough questions:
Can the earth survive the economy of men?
Are our leaders bottom feeders who sell our children
for power and short-term gain?
Never mind the pain of tomorrow's child

the milder weather melting the polar ice, the stench
of dying oceans and lakes, the high stakes
of the games they are playing with our survival
the dice they are rolling in their mine games

I sing the family farm, denounce the shit factories
the regimes of mining kings
I sing the last clear waters, home to ancient
sturgeon, to trout and otters, waters that feeds
Bad River's sons and daughters, that run
above a blacksnake now
I sing the water warriors, the indigenous tribes
who fight for the lives of all our kin
I sing for the water without and within
because we all are formed of water and stars
I sing for all who stand tall as the battle
to save our water begins.

Our children should not die for our sins.

Only Rob

Welcome to the Poem Farm

(For Walt Whitman)

Drink of clear waters; feed from the Earth.
Neither war nor commerce may find you here.
Feast with me in body, spirit, in love and whimsy.
Walk barefoot, head to toe; feed from rows of peas.
You must kill the white noise with wind song,
with the giggling rain, with the laughter of unencumbered
souls, and hyjinks of aged children, electric words
herded into the folds of opened minds.

Read not from my tired pen, but from the lines
on callused hands, the face of the generous land,
the voices in the forest that rise with stars and moon.
You will know that this is not my place, but I am of it.
You are of it, and we will ripen with the apples, plums.
You will find deeper answers to the poignant question
of the owl; hear a flute sing with loons, the voice
of the world in an ever changing symphony of celebration.

Don't be a poet, but a poem; follow prophets, not profits;
choose a wave in green aurora and surf it to the lands
behind the moon; dance with fairies and playful gnomes.
Nothing is impossible until you name it such.

There are poems in hummingbirds, in the dappled dog,
the weeding woman, the crescendo of wailing wolves.
There is an entire book of them in the stream, a library
of them in the gardens, a peaceful revolution brewing

on the porch. Welcome; there is electricity here; just plug in your umbilical cord and go for a walk.

Only Rob

Paula Tohline Calhoun

My life, as for everyone, is a day-to-day proposition, and I am grateful for it all. I love to write and spend most of my time doing it or thinking about doing it. A brief glimpse into my life is the little parody-trifle below, which in some ways describes my life indoors. I am unable to venture outside much, so I write about it from memory. I have some wonderful ones. IPC is a dynamic group and has offered me a great outlet for expression in addition to serving up some good poetry by which to be entertained, enlightened, and inspired.

CAN YOU SEE ME NOW?

(Or, A snapshot of how my mind wanders)

I think I'd rather write a poem
about some trees than stand below 'em.
They are indeed a joy to see
but during storms, no place to be.
For lightning's electricity

is deadly when it strikes a tree.
Unless of course you're wearing sneakers,
(the shoe of choice for shelter seekers).
If clouds appear on the horizon
(which you should always keep your eyes on),
look for shelter where you'll be
safer than beneath a tree.
Perhaps it's best to stay indoors
(the better space for you and yours).
Odes to trees can best be written
inside, with a comfy chair to sit in.
Through my window, I can see
a place of shade beneath a tree.
As tempting as that spot may be
I'll stay indoors, with good A.C.

À la recherché du temps perdu

So much of living is accomplished
without a word of notice, or a sigh
from those who live it. But reflections
of yesterday, mirrored in the now
add the memorable to the once mundane.
A soft chamois of sweet recollection
can burnish the dullest of moments.
Poetry is the afterglow of times past.

Les temps perdu must be revisited,
fallen petals rejoined to the blossom,
a swan's wake must first kiss the shore,
and tears must be shed, to be recounted.
The glory of poetry is the aftermath.
Joy and sorrow gain their weighty remembrance,
are restored to new life in the act of restoration.
Beauty unnoticed can be redeemed
only in thoughtful memory. To set aside
a single day for wonder is a fool's errand.

Poetry is extracted from the heart over time;
in due consideration for all that is believed,
the what-have-yous of practiced retrospect.
It is found in the selected words, precious coins
minted from yesterday's silver and gold.

Paula Tohline Calhoun

Square Peg Considers Her Métier, and Ponders the Alternatives

I wonder," said Square Peg to round hole,
"Are you the space for me?"
"It depends," said the hole, and added,
"Give me a try and see."
"From what I observe of your configuration,
whether I'll fit is in doubt,"
said Peg to the hole. The hole responded,
"If you're just looking, you'll never find out."
"But you don't understand," whined Peg, in defense,
"I'm a square; I'm not shaped for you!"
"Squares can change, you could adapt,"
said the hole, "If you wanted to."
"Besides," hole noted, "fitting in is not always
just what it's cracked up to be.
There's a certain 'je ne sais quoi'
in a life of nonconformity."
Quietly, Square Peg pondered
the ways of a well-rounded life:
"Perhaps, with the aid of a hammer,
and some whittling from a knife,
I'll find, once I live a while in the round,
and I put my old habits behind me,
though life won't be perfect, I'll never be bored
if I let go the square ties that bind me."

Paula Tohline Calhoun

Still I Fly

In my dreams
I fly again, rushing downhill
bracing energizing
cold air slaps color
on my face, and
I look up and out
over eternity of sky
mountains trees.
Parallel blades slice
crisp and sharp
into new powdered ice--
the only sound above the wind.
Time stops, I race through
leaving behind me a curly
blue ribbon the wind carries away.
In my dreams, still,
ageless, singular, free
I fly.

Paula Tohline Calhoun

Poet Prolific

I am James Nichols aka PoetProlific. I am a 51 year old father of five great kids and husband to a wife whom I owe my very existence. She's my conscience when I lose it, my sanity, my rational mind, and the love of my life. I am, by trade, an ER doctor for the last 25 years, genuine, board certified and still in active practice. I have a new position for the last year and it's been a great and much needed transition and career saver. My interests are diverse; from sports to philosophy and witting is my passion. It got me through a dark part of my life and it's so nice to be in a good place now. I try to write daily, and eventually want to publish and write a book or two. My poems run the gamut from rhyme to free verse to prose. I have met some fascinating friends on AP and am much honored to participate in this publication.

An Old Man's Prayer

"Why do kids
and a few dogs, too
pray to the God
they thought they knew?

Some will grow
find a wife.
Some will die
too young in life.

So this same God
who answers prayers
kills kids and pets?
Doesn't seem fair"

But the old man says,
"Don't count him out.
God is there.
There is no doubt.

I saw him once
in a boy your age.
Both folks dead
as the fire raged.

He cried for weeks
He tried to die.
But God said, "No!",
and I'll tell you why.

You see that boy
became a man.
And had a son,
part of God's plan.

Then that son made
a little boy
and like his dad,
provided joy."

And the old man prays,
says God is great.
His life's complete
and he's running late.

"Soon God calls
and I'll be done.
I hope by then
you have a son.

For I'm the man
now old and gray.
You'd not be here
had I not prayed.

I hated God,
for He had lied.
Alone I planned
my suicide.

The loaded gun
and finished note
in front of me
when God spoke.

He told me, 'Wait,
you have to live.
There's a little boy
you need to give

the gift of life
before you depart
So close your eyes,
open your heart.'

And here I am
with my grandson.
And now, you see,
my life is done."

With that he smiled
and closed his eyes.
Eternity held
the final prize.

That little boy
cried that day.
And when he stopped,
began to pray.

His prayer is simple,
and his heart is true,

"Grant me wisdom, God,
to follow you."

PoetProlific

Daily Encore

Rain-grey days are the worst
for his presentation.
Weather's distraction
steals his thoughts
as it stills his soul.

Most days the others ignore
him, busy with their own
productions.
He is the only one who reads.

Others seem to sit and speak softly
to a polite and punctual
audience.

So he writes daily:
terse exclamations of love,
heated arguments with angels
and demons,
and even sad love songs,
but he never sings.
He only reads
with a broken voice
that mirrors his heart.

He's alone today with her
and she's ignoring him
as he finishes his latest work,
"...in eternity, love's a constant."
Silence, the passive killer of hope,

the enemy of every performer, ensues
as he folds the paper and tucks
it into his coat.

The rain taps lightly about his feet
as he kneels and kisses
the cold granite headstone
of the only true fan
he ever had.

PoetProlific

Fall For It

Ochre becomes her
when shadows precede dusk's demise.
Crisp crunch of tip toes
betrays her strategy.
Jaundiced leaves relinquish summer's grip,
surrendering to the chilled wind-knives
as suicide jumpers spiral upon the pile.

She is silent and supine,
a bed of deadness billows about.
Her ochre now home among the yellow friends,
she remarks on the symbolism
of the dead leaf pile as a bed
and her desire to escape.
A casual glance at her erupting smile
tells me I've been duped again
by my lady who stifles a laugh
as she promises resurrection by spring.

PoetProlific

R J Kram

A Small Biography

When he was younger, R.J. Kram enjoyed fishing with his Grandfather above almost anything. Come heavy wind or torrential rain, it did not matter. Give him a fishing rod and his Grandfather and he would stay out there for days if he were able. Memories of those lakes and rivers continue to influence him and his writing to this day.

He had started writing poetry when he was 16 years old thanks to a high school creative writing project. He had always enjoyed poetry and had an inclination towards it thanks to his father, whose writing is another source of great influence. As he has grown and matured so has his work and his muse has been ever more active. His work tends to center around, though certainly not limited to, emotions and past personal events frequently expressed through the use of nature metaphors.

Outside of writing, R.J. likes to build/fix computers and works as an I.T. Technician who is very passionate about technology and helping others understand it. He is a loving father of two beautiful girls and husband to an amazing and caring wife. They are often the subject in several of his more personal pieces about love and life.

A drink to regret

Mint julep
swirls through
my teeth
smooth
as it goes down

one too many
words spoken
by alcohol

this tired summer sun
punishes me
a raisin
in a world
of mixed nuts

ice cubes kiss
the bottom of the glass

empty

I close my eyes
on cherry dusk
and dream of winter

RJ Kram

Watching Snow Flakes

My fence posts
brim white
with flakes of snow

which dance
down between
yellow maples
as they groan
in the soft breeze

their ballet brings
the warmth of dimples
to my cheeks

but soon the leaves
will brown

and I'll feel
the icy whisper
of aging
once again

RJ Kram

Gone too soon

I lie here
silent

ragged hide
draped
on this weathered log
as chin and belly
press
into its grain

at home
among the
lavender butterflies
that once
lit your eyes

I feel you
in the soft rock
of the river

and hear you
in the breeze
rustling
willow leaves

shaking a few loose
to ripple
and swirl

in the cool water
with me

RJ Kram

Scott Waters

Native son of Indiana, Chicago and New York City knockabout, former starving Greenpeace canvasser, long-time resident of Berkeley and Oakland, loving husband, father of an 8-year-old son, neutral bringer of peace, love, and harmony to labor-management relations, singer-songwriter, and one-time poet who stared too long and too impractically into the poetic abyss at age 22, I am now a grateful middle-ager enjoying an unexpected literary renaissance thanks to allpoetry.com and twenty-minute train rides to work armed with a pen, a notebook, and a crackerjack imagination that finally learned how to chew up the scenery without devouring its host.

Outside the box

down the long undulating tunnel
slides a spirit,
landing with a thud
inside a warm, sterile box.

the spirit is taken home
to a softer box,
where it is rocked inside
an even smaller box,
smiling and whimpering
in formless dreams.

the spirit plays in
cardboard boxes
and sandboxes,
gazing open-mouthed
at pigeons circling
the spire of the courthouse
beyond a grove of sycamores.

all too soon the spirit
is sent to be educated
in a large rectangular box,
where it becomes adept
at drawing perfect squares and cubes
and other inferior
and soon forgotten shapes.

spirit graduates from one box
into another, and another,
walking across the squared-off
campus to where it sleeps
in a shared box
with another baffled spirit,
peering together at raindrops
meandering down the window,
the lush wash of sycamores
bending beyond the glass.

spirit leaves the learning box
and boxes itself into
a large up-ended
shoebox of a building,
stares at a glowing box
10 hours a day
(taking a break at noon
for a nice box lunch),
then drives a wheeled box
to the box store to buy
a box of chocolates
for its box-crazy spouse,
but first stops
for a quick workout
at a sprawling box
near the mall -- staring up,
panting, at a colorful box
on the wall and the flickering
ghosts of other spirits
trapped inside their boxy lives.

decades pass.

a hollow body is laid to rest
inside its final box,
eased into the supple ground
with the rippling worms
and tangled roots
of sycamores
tossing their brown heads
in the cold autumn air above,

while a liberated spirit glides along
the ample hip of the ancient,
curvaceous Earth.

Scott Waters

If a brick wall in Chicago could talk

when I was 22
    I tried to dance
  with poetry
       and ended up
     with singed eyebrows
       blistered fingers
  a lost career
    and a desert of loneliness
      stretching from
    my front door

because poetry
    was not content
  to dance
      it wanted
    to consume the tinder
   of my very cells
   till there was
     nothing left of me
  but cinders of ink
      smudged in notebooks
    stacked on a desk
     beside a window
  with a view
    of a brick wall

and the wall observed
    the fiery drama

inside the kiln
    of that studio apartment

and said nothing

    the sunlight reaching down
        into the grey canyon
            between buildings
    for 20 minutes each day
    to reveal how black
the bricks had become
    from simply
        bearing witness

to my consummation.

Scott Waters

persimmon

one bite
through crisp skin

    and you are running
in an orchard
hiding from the seeker
with your parents
and grandparents
    somewhere out of view
their voices murmuring
through the settling dusk
talking of tractors and peat moss

footsteps come near
you climb
    into the nearest tree
and wait for the hollering voices
of children
to pass

when they have gone
you notice
the plump little
    orange-ochre
    pumpkin replica
suspended inches
from your nose

your small fist opens

encloses the smooth sheen

pulls

and with one bite
through crisp skin
    you are in your kitchen
the kids hollering in the backyard
your parents and grandparents
murmuring in their picture frames

past present and future
bobbing on the river

of your tongue

Scott Waters

Shelby Simmons

To all of you who have found this book in your hands, who happen to be open to this page I'm honored you're here, and I hope that feeling is reciprocated. If not, I'm still honored, and I hope I can change your mind.

Shelby Simmons (that's me!) is (at the time of writing this, unfortunately I am a victim of linear time) a 19 year old wannabe poet, who writes some things sometimes, some things that may or may not be classified as poetry, and has genuinely good people believing that this writing is worth reading. So that's something. Shelby is from beautiful British Columbia, born and raised, and has always taken a liking to the arts. Still reading? Wow, I commend you.

Some things that Shelby is:

•Really passionate about poetry. No really. I'm not messing around. "Abandon all other commitments because the

Canadian International Poetry Slam is happening and I must volunteer at every event" - kind of passionate.
• An educator, performer, and over-all empathizer.
• A superhero on the weekends (shhh).

Some things that Shelby is not:
• Organized.
• Chill, in any form of the word.
• Organized.

Taxi Services Don't Send Spaceships

You hitchhiked home
from the rings of Saturn
on a passing comet.
We always knew
you would inevitably leave,
leaving me with
a pocket of waterlogged
bus tickets,
silver lips
and dark matter making home,
making home,
in my stomach.

You couldn't handle
my shaking voice
as we stared into the galaxy
that seemed emptier
in the eclipse
(I have grown accustomed to).
I can't say I blame you
for my shaking hands,
for the way gravity pulls
my heart to my feet,
for the oxygen that is
running low.

I can't be nervous
when my only company
is the paranoia
that lives in the spacesuit
you called
coping mechanisms.
You placed a constellation
in the sky,
begging me to keep you out
of the narrative.

How,
when the bus tickets
are pointless,
yet
my last connection
to Earth,
my lifeline
to you
(if I ever come home).

Shelby Simmons

April 14 (A poem)

I am not
     (a poem).

I do not exist in the
scribbles on the back
of napkins, finger painting
in the fogged windows
of your rusted Volkswagen.
Ellipses after what would
usually be a sentence end...

You once compared the wind
to my breath, as if your neck
was land I treaded and
claimed, and goodbyes were
characterized like poorly timed line
breaks.
I never consented.

It took me too long to realize
what dehumanization
meant, when you constrain
a poet into the shackles
of their poetry. I do not have
paper skin or ink tears.

I am not
     (a poem).

Shelby Simmons

This body writes poetry also

i. jaw

your knuckles memorized
every sharp edge,
your thumbs pressed
into my face
as if to render up
contour until
I was hollow enough
for you;
you whispered eulogies
into my mouth
to stifle
siren screams.

ii. spine

your fingerprints claimed
this mountain range
of rubble
and chronic pain.
you handled the fossils
with fine instruments,
but never thought to ask
if the land you treaded
was sacred;
trespassing
on fragile earth.

iii. waist

you carved your handprints
into the skin
where you figured
your hands could fall asleep,
beneath my ribs,
petit, yet soft...
at the very least
disquieting.
I have never been
a mannequin
for such violent displays.

iv. knees

you cut crude incisions
along my hinges,
hiding there the nebulas
of lies painted
dark purple, blue, green.
I bruise easily,
and when I scar,
my body reflects
the gravel
you forced me
to kneel on
at the altar
you called forgiveness.

Shelby Simmons

Skylar7

Chloe H. (Skylar7) is a student in Malaysia now pursuing a degree in creative writing. She has loved stories from a young age and has been writing since age 9. For her, writing is a form of catharsis.

Poems, prose and plays all tell raw stories, exposing the truth with a beautiful lie.

Walking Mirrors

I have realized,
forefathers,
whether willful or otherwise,
assemble our fragments
till smooth panes are forged
adorned with reused design.

And we – nothing
but wandering depictions
expiring with time.

Skylar7

2nd Degree Burns

Scale the turrets of inferno,
feel as the tongues lick up
traces of you.
From threads of clothes left astray,
reaching the crusts of your being.

Feel the panic in your chest
choke you
more than the exhalations of fire.

Feel your head swim from suffocation
muscles heavy,
like you are drowning under water.

And when water does come
to grant you mercy,
the agony doubles back, bounding.
Tragic really;
you were just short
of third degree.

Skylar7

Deforestation

No matter the courage,
if teeth dare graze
the thickest skin of bark,
even if leaves hold fast
even if roots ground them,
if teeth dare graze,
it is only a matter of time
that the trunk gives way,
its resolve withering,
slamming its head on its own feet
and falls asleep
even under the brightest sun.

How the mighty have fallen
and still fall.
As long as chainsaws
do not grow cavities,
the mighty will continue to fall.
No matter the courage.

Skylar7

Socalalto

Marcy Wingard (aka Socalalto) is an ancient hippy chick who came of age in the 60's as an English Major. She wrote short stories and poetry during her college years and sang her way from childhood into "adulthood" including a stint as a folk singer at Midwestern Hootenannies and an 18 year gig in Oaks Chamber Singers, a local chamber choir.

The world intruded and husbands, children and working got in the way of writing. After her husband's untimely death 12 years ago - she started writing seriously again though mostly for herself, not sharing the product with anyone.

Discovering AP in 2013, she really started honing her craft and letting others see what she was writing. Finally about 2 years ago, she began to attend poetry events, read her work and became a part of the local poetry community. Even more recently, she joined IPC and has thoroughly enjoyed writing for the contests of Elegia, Becki Friend, Monarch and others in this group.

For nearly 40 years she has resided in Southern California, about 50 miles northwest of Los Angeles. Writing poetry is a way to release creativity and express feelings and ideas that she doesn't verbalize. She writes poetry about nature, observations of daily life and poems that express feelings.

Silverberry is Lavender Blue

Now that he's dead, I can paint the house
He always wanted everything white,
the angles square and Danish simple
like the plain birch box his ashes fill

I'm tired of white walls – it's color I crave
around me drowning out the grief
Bright color, shades that soften gently
the angled primness of modern space

Something to help block out his loss
To stop my constant thoughts of him
That we won't sit on rocking chairs,
grow old together in dimming light

Victorian Mauve behind the bed -
I see him spinning in his grave
"O my God, not pink - never pink"
Chenille for the other bedroom walls

Luscious, Amazon Moss for kitchen color,
A bit of Desert Caravan, Cracked Wheat
spice up the powder room, but best of all
Silverberry graces the master bathroom wall!

Socalalto

Shadow Cat

Shadow - arranged at my feet, licking his paws,
lush, deep gray fur, in disarray
as he cleans between his claws
Stretched out full length, back arched

Gracefully outstretched, intent on his task
Steely green eyes staring back at me
Rumbling purr, audible from three feet away
eyelids close as he relaxes, purring continues

Sunlight glints down from the window
he rolls over on his back, extending
well-shaped legs - now his cat dance
is kneading the carpet

Content in his afternoon reverie,
sudden sound from the hall catches his ear
and he's off like a flash to check it out
A moment passes, he's back, hits his bowl

A couple of bits of kibble is enough,
Nonchalant - he licks his whiskers delicately
then falls at my feet, rubbing against my legs,
loudly purring his contentment with life

He stares up at me and springs deftly
up onto my lap in one graceful leap
rubbing his head against my knee -
purring is even louder now

Stretching out his paw, he reaches the keyboard
I bat his leg away from the computer
he settles back, the rumbling even and deep
Shadow is content and his world is complete.

Socalalto

Winter Woods Waiting

Stark sentinels - once proud with leafy dress
stand silent, gaunt, spare and grim
stooped - facing the pale winter sun
naked in November light

Cold, white coverlet blankets the spaces,
surface undulates with knobs and piles, humps
of shattered logs, dead leaves hidden, softened
broken by slender branches

Contrast of white and gray-black -
animal tracks break the crust of white,
tiny rounded holes sunk into the frozen ground
reminding the woods of what still lives

Winter woods, sleep restlessly - waiting for spring
remembers the young pale green of delicate leaves
just opening, the full heavy foliage of summer's grandeur
the riot of fall - orange, yellow, brown - crackling

And then - quiet, wary, winter steals in on the wind
takes over the woods, settling over all
creeping in with deadening silence, the living world stops
world of frozen silence waits.

Socalalto

Tuni

Madhu Singh is a fledgling poet and eternal optimist who believes someday poetry will pay the bills. She reigns over a make-belief kingdom around the plains of New Delhi. She loves to write short stories and poetry and dabbles in free-verse and English language haiku.

Water Hyacinth

I long to lose myself in something;
a hyacinth floating on the surface,
I want to forget myself in the element of water.

To hear in the soft gurgle of a brook
tales it happily chatters to the woods
and know the secret joy it speaks of.

To rest like a pebble in the deep water-bed,
discover its secret of staying still
in the ever flowing current.

To flow with the breeze whistling through silver-oaks
bringing warmth from lands afar,
find what it seeks in its never ending journey.

To drink with wood-nymphs from streams,
wondering if thirst ever quenches
and if water always tastes sweet.

I wish to ask that hyacinth
where its fragrance went.

Tuni

Januaryscape

In the hinterland
between Yamuna's sluggish pause
and the far-edge of the desert
deep winter is stale henna
coned on palms and feet;
patches of fleshy earth
peeking through dried, intricate
patterns of scrub.

A bleak world, its beauty banished
as if to let the dead visage speak
before the redeeming portents of spring
overwhelm its paler truth.

Tuni

I'm waiting for #86 by Café Fariyas

A pavement coconut-seller
hacks the green fibrous shell in a flourish,
slakes the summer off parched throats
and July blows in from the dock
pillioned with an odour of rotting fish.

With a lurch I am reminded of the buffaloes:
tethered by their snouts to the temple's courtyard,
priests sprinkling water from banyan leaves
on their ears for a token of assent,
their foreheads smeared with turmeric-vermillion paste,
the air rent with their ferrous baying.

I walk up to Aldrin in the bar
and order a pint of Kingfisher.

Tuni

Word Gatherer

Bobbie Jean Wright, aka Word Gatherer, was born in rural Georgia in 1977, the oldest of eight children. She began writing at the age if nine after falling in love with Edgar Allan Poe. Her favorite place to write has always been an old porch swing or beneath her favorite oak, preferably in the fall of the year.

Bobbie spent most of her preteens traveling up and down the east coast, after her parents' divorce. She returned to rural Georgia at the age of thirteen where she has resided since. She married the love of her life at twenty four and they are raising her heart, their two beautiful daughters.

As she has matured, so has her taste in poetry. Her favorite poet is Pablo Neruda; his work strongly influences her own. She has many favorites on Allpoetry.com (most of whom are members of the Indelible Poetry Club) where you can read more of her work.

Bobbie has no college education. Her writing comes from a natural spring inside her that flows from her love of words and desire to manipulate their meaning. She had one book of poetry published in 2005 "Wild as the Southern Wind" through Publish America and desires to publish more in the future.

My Spirit Weeps the Wailing of a Thousand Years

Your leaving is as if I have died. Night's great foot burdens my soul until it runs screaming to yours; my spirit weeps the wailing of a thousand years. I cannot conceal my love for you. It haunts my days and groans through my nights.

No time will ever come when your voice does not echo within the hallways of my living and burst without into this foggy graveyard where I now reside.

I've loved you so that these thousand years have no recollection of us ever being two separate entities, for where you are, my blue agile darling, there is my love. It envelopes you in the slivers of moonlight, as you envelope and detain me, without even your knowledge.

Our love is so meant to be that neither time nor distance can separate its truth. My darling there is a gaping wound in my voice that bleeds your name. A floral odor rises from my skin that sings of your flesh. My fingertips are lonely keys seeking the locks of your hair.

Even the steel claws of death that grip and hold me now, cannot stamp out the beam of light that will join the moon to forever worship your loveliness.

Word Gatherer

The Essence of Your Soul

How I long to touch
what is impalpable…
the essence of your soul,
but it conspires with light
to run away.

I bend to you at morning
as you stow away in
the warmth of the sun…
only to burn through my day.

I am reduced to hope
that night will fold me
in the blanket of your eyes.

When it does,
I kneel to your essence
to worship, without abandon
the desire you create within me.

You have stolen my heart,
I cannot live without it.

Word Gatherer

Collection

At 5 am,
I exfoliate your memory
with coffee, cigarettes and words
flowing from my fingertips...
my morning ritual.
My spinning brings gold
that would rival Rumpelstiltskin's
collection of souls and wealth,
allowing the sunlight to glimmer
upon my face in shining wonder.
The day does pass, however,
and night visions make certain
your ontogeny returns
to abandon my happiness
...slow my heart.
Some day-breaks discover me
...lying naked and barely breathing...
for the smothering cover of you.
I drag through the murk
to massage away the sadness
through another caffeine and nicotine
(black and white)
honoring of your memory
(knowing it is not the end
...never the end).

You have a collection yourself
...even if you're unaware...
of trophies lining the walls
in my poetic dungeon.
Maybe you could walk the halls
...and find happiness there.

Word Gatherer

Made in the USA
Middletown, DE
21 December 2016